1117 IN ICELAND AND ENGLAND

By
PETER FOOTE

EMERITUS PROFESSOR OF SCANDINAVIAN STUDIES
IN THE UNIVERSITY OF LONDON

*The Dorothea Coke Memorial Lecture
in Northern Studies
delivered at University College London
14 March 2002*

PUBLISHED FOR THE COLLEGE BY THE
VIKING SOCIETY FOR NORTHERN RESEARCH
LONDON

© UNIVERSITY COLLEGE LONDON 2003

ISBN: 0 903521 59 8

PRINTED BY SHORT RUN PRESS LIMITED EXETER

1117 IN ICELAND AND ENGLAND[1]

A MAN IN HIS DOTAGE HAS FEW UNTRIED ORATORICAL DEVICES left to him in attempting to capture the benevolence of an audience. Acknowledging defeat in the struggle for novelty, I fall back on an old anecdote. It has the advantage first of unimpeachable authority, for it was recorded by Dean Ramsay of Edinburgh in his *Reminiscences of Scottish Life and Character*, published in 1857; and the advantage second of remarkable aptness to my present circumstances. The Dean tells of a Highland hamlet cut off by snow for weeks on end. Tobacco supplies were exhausted and the minister of the parish, an inveterate snuff-taker, was in desperate straits. He at last sent his beadle through the snow to find what he could; all in vain – he came back empty-handed. The despondent minister made a final appeal. Struck by a sudden thought, the beadle left him, only to return a few minutes later with a well-filled box. The wordless minister took a long, deep pinch. Then asked where he had got it. To which came the reply, "I soupit the poupit" – "I swept the pulpit."

I can say much the same of this paper, a miscellany, I fear, as dry as old snuff, though perhaps the more desperately tolerant among you will find some small savour still in a few grains. Despite this dismal outlook, I shall at least endeavour not to emulate that elderly peer of the realm who dreamt he was making a speech in the House of Lords and woke up to find that that was precisely what he was doing.

I feel it proper however to begin by saying something about the origins of this memorial lectureship. I am particularly moved to do so because I am pretty certainly the only surviving member of

---

[1] This lecture is printed almost exactly as it was delivered, with a few footnotes added where documentation seemed most called for. The knowledgeable reader will readily see where I tread boldly on thin ice. I am grateful to Michael Barnes for his help as general editor.

the College who had any personal acquaintance with Colonel Coke, and heard from him a little – not much for he was a modest, reticent man – about his pious motive.

Colonel B. E. Coke, born in 1884, came of landed gentry in Derbyshire.[2] His army career was with the Royal Engineers, from whom he retired after good service in the first war with the rank of Lieutenant-Colonel. After a year or so he went up to Clare College, Cambridge, to read Natural Sciences, graduating in 1922 at the age of thirty-eight. As far as I know, he then settled down to manage family affairs. They seem to have prospered and latterly he certainly had both the fortune and the leisure to travel and to fish. He combined these pastimes in a commendably sensible way by going northward, to Shetland, Iceland, Norway. His wife, Dorothea (they had married in 1907), went with him and one time in Norway, while he fished up in Namdalen, she took an interest in the antiquities round about and became fascinated by the stories, quite likely tall stories, told her by a local guide about his Viking ancestors, whose burial mounds were still there to be seen in the landscape. So fascinated, indeed, that in her last years she read and wrote and talked about Vikings and their impact on England, subjects which, in her circle at least, she felt to be quite unduly neglected. When she died in 1952 Colonel Coke looked for a memorial which would foster the interests she had pursued with such enthusiasm. Not unnaturally, he turned to Cambridge and consultation there led to the establishment in 1954 of the Dorothea Coke Fund, whose purpose, as now defined, "shall be to promote the publication of original work on the early history of the Scandinavian countries". For nearly half a century the Fund has been of great benefit to authors and publishers, and since it is in a healthy condition – so I am told – will doubtless continue to be. I say this in spite of the feeling I sometimes have that a fund which would pay some authors not to publish would also be a good institution.

It was through the Fund that first the Viking Society and then our Department of Scandinavian Studies came to know Colonel Coke. In 1957 the Society undertook to publish an important

---

[2] Burke's *Landed Gentry* (18th ed., 1965), 147–49 (Coke of Brookhill).

monograph, *Dating the Icelandic Sagas*, by Einar Ólafur Sveinsson, translated by Gabriel Turville-Petre. The Society was of course short of cash and a subvention was sought from the Cambridge Fund. The managers were sympathetic but unable to help because an article of the donation agreement limited their support to work by British authors. It was however suggested that a personal approach might be made to Colonel Coke. Now Hugh Smith, of blessed memory, Quain Professor of English at the time, was also Director of Scandinavian Studies in the College and, with Gabriel Turville-Petre, Honorary Secretary of the Viking Society, while I was Reader in the Scandinavian Department and Assistant Secretary of the Society. Hugh had a happy solution to many problems: "Let us have a lunch," he would say. So we had a lunch with Colonel Coke as our guest, and, as usual, enough wine flowed to ensure that talk flowed too. Colonel Coke made a private donation towards publication of Einar's monograph. It came out in 1958, and the verso of the half-title page bears an inscription: "The publication of this volume has been made possible by a gift in memory of Dorothea Coke", followed by three lines of verse, frankly sentimental, recalling magical fishing days in West Iceland:

> But the whimbrel still are calling
> And the silver water's falling
> Just where Langá River joins the sea.

I kept in touch with Colonel Coke thereafter, and one day, needless to say over lunch, the notion of this memorial lecture was born. Agreement was easily reached with the College, Colonel Coke firmly admonishing the College authorities to do all in their power to maintain the value of the capital he contributed – astonishingly enough, this appears to have happened. It was intended that stress should lie on early Anglo-Scandinavian relations, reinforced by the proviso that lectures should be given alternately by a homebred scholar and one invited from the Northern world. The first in the series in 1963, when Norman Garmonsway spoke on Canute, king of England, Denmark and Norway, was a happy choice; and with a couple of exceptions the English element in the performance has been dutifully maintained. The lectures were not established as calendar fixtures – this is now the seventeenth – and you may have noticed that I managed to squeeze England into my title. As happens often enough in this imperfect world, that title had to be submitted long before I had much idea of the substance of my talk: I have always had sympathy for the querulous remark attributed, I think, to W. B. Yeats: "How can I tell what I mean till I've heard what I've said?" But I should make it plain at this point that 1117 in England and 1117 in Iceland represent a coincidence, not a connection, a coincidence though which may permit some comparison and more especially some contrast. The laws of early Iceland are my main topic. As a species of literature and as a fount of historical information at various cultural levels students and scholars alike tend to find these problematic, intractable, amorphous, even mysterious. Discussion which may help to throw light on their nature is, or ought to be, welcome. Or so I hope.

So I start with 1117 in Iceland. That summer was Bergþórr Hrafnsson's first summer as Lawspeaker, and at the General Assembly

> the novel resolution was taken to write our laws in a book at Hafliði Másson's during the coming winter, following the account and counsel of Hafliði and Bergþórr and other wise men selected for the task. They were to make all the new-law proposals that seemed to them better than the old laws. The proposals were to be announced in the Law Council the following summer and all those kept to which the majority of the Law Council men did not object. And it came about in due course that *Vígslóði* and much else in the laws were written and read out next summer by clerics in the Law Council. And all were content with that and no one made any objection to it.

This well-known passage from Ari Þorgilsson's *Íslendingabók*[3] was written within ten years or so of the event – we need have no doubt of its accuracy and we may be glad to have it. Ari doubtless included this information because he saw written law as a sign of national maturity, a statement of national identity, and found it needless to give the further details we would have welcomed. How many and who were the other experts consulted? What was written besides *Vígslóði*? What was read out in the Law Council in 1118 – the whole of *Vígslóði* and "much else in the laws" or only the novelties that improved the earlier regulations – and were men reminded what those earlier rules were? One thing we can be certain

---

[3] *Íslendingabók*, ch. 10; ed. Jakob Benediktsson, Íslenzk Fornrit I (1968), 23–24.

of is that there was a discrete section of the laws, *Vígslóði*, which dealt with homicide and related matters; and if that was the case, there were doubtless other discrete sections dealing with other affairs. The arrangement of the laws was an organised arrangement.

The codification begun in the winter of 1117 may have been continued but no source confirms that it was. Nevertheless the work that resulted from the deliberations of those law-learned men existed in a manuscript which was apparently accorded official status and was referred to as *Hafliðaskrá*, Hafliði's screed; we can of course assume that it existed in other copies as well. We know about its official status from a provision in the so-called Law Council Section of the laws, which defines the authority enjoyed by different law records; the provision most probably dates from the latter half of the twelfth century, and the framers of it then regarded Hafliði's screed, as far as it went, as authoritative.[4] The provision presupposes however that other law records might disagree with it – in that case they were either adulterated transcripts or records obtained from other men, whose memories were quite possibly stocked with laws different in form or content, or both, from those of the Hafliði revision. They may even have been derived from pre-Hafliði written sources, for it is not out of the way to suppose that laws were recorded in Iceland before 1117, recorded but not codified. By 1117 Icelanders had been Christian for over a century. In that time the essential work of education had been undertaken by foreign bishops and then by the native bishops, Ísleifr Gizurarson and his son, Gizurr, and men closely associated with them and their family. Two of the missionary bishops both spent nineteen or twenty years in Iceland and their subsequent careers showed they were churchmen of distinction: the one left in 1049 and became abbot of Abingdon in Berkshire, the other left in 1067 and became bishop of Selje in Norway, the precursor of the see of Bergen.[5] They were certainly familiar with written law and

---

[4] *Grágás* I, Første Del, ed. Vilhjálmur Finsen (1852; reprinted with *Grágás* II and III, 1974), 213; *Laws of Early Iceland* I, tr. Andrew Dennis, Peter Foote, Richard Perkins (1980), 190–91.

[5] Oluf Kolsrud, *Den norske Kirkes Erkebiskoper og Biskoper indtil Reformationen*, Diplomatarium Norvegicum XVII:B (1913), 197.

the same can be said of Ísleifr and Gizurr. These, father and son, had both been to school in Germany, Ísleifr from childhood till after ordination as priest, Gizurr we don't know how long. They may not have known Frankish law-texts but they were obviously acquainted with church law in various forms, Pseudo-Isidore perhaps or even Burchard's great *Decretum*, completed in just those years that Ísleifr spent at Herford in Westfalen and apparently put into rapid circulation; or at least some of Burchard's many sources, capitulary and canon collections and penitentials, not forgetting that ultimate source, Scripture itself. And in any case law was undoubtedly being written in Norway in their time, though opinions differ on whether that recording began before or after about 1050.[6] Preserved among the *Grágás* laws is an attestation to the terms of a pact believed to have been made between the Icelanders and St Óláfr of Norway. King Óláf's effective rule was from 1015 to 1028, but the attestation almost certainly dates from 1083, when Bishop Gizurr was on his way home from consecration at the pope's behest in Magdeburg.[7] It would be absurd to think that in that circle and those circumstances the articles of the pact then affirmed were not documented.

The provision which referred to Hafliði's screed gives prime authority to the lawbooks kept at the cathedral establishments of Skálholt and Hólar, with ultimate precedence given to the one at Skálholt, the centre of the senior and larger diocese. This enactment has been compared to the so-called Citation Laws of late antiquity, the most important of them issued by the emperors Theodosius and Valentinianus in 426, which laid down a similar ordering of legal authority.[8] The need for such regulation is reckoned to be the confusion that arose from conflicting law records and jurists'

---

[6] Cf. Magnus Rindal in *Den eldre Gulatingslova*, ed. Bjørn Eithun, Magnus Rindal, Tor Ulset; Riksarkivet, Norrøne tekster nr. 6 (1994), 9–12.

[7] *Grágás* I, Anden Del, ed. Vilhjálmur Finsen (1852), 195–97; *Laws of Early Iceland* II, tr. Andrew Dennis, Peter Foote, Richard Perkins (2000), 210–13. Gizur's consecration in Magdeburg was a papal move in the strife between Gregory VII and emperor Henry IV; cf. D. Claude, *Geschichte des Erzbistums Magdeburg* I (1972), 349–79.

[8] See "Some lines in *Lögréttuþáttr*" in Peter Foote, *Aurvandilstá* (1984), 155–64.

opinions. From this it is natural to infer the existence of much written law in twelfth-century Iceland, and not all of it coherently univocal. Whole lawbooks may have been rare, though there were men wealthy enough to commission them, but separate sections of particular everyday concern, procedural rules, formula collections, may have been commonplace. We remember that about 1150 or not long afterwards the First Grammarian urged the utility of his orthographic system as a help towards reading and writing and put laws first in his list of what was now written and read.[9] Although this was an age of script, there is of course no need to think that learning law by heart was a thing of the past. Stories make a theme of boys learning law from mentors, Gunnlaugr ormstunga from Þorsteinn Egilsson, Sigmundr Leifsson from Þrándr í Götu; and in 1221 Gizurr Þorvaldsson precociously prosecuted a case at the General Assembly at the age of twelve – it is unlikely that he needed a book.[10]

It will come as no surprise to you to learn that almost everything I have said so far cannot be backed by first-hand contemporary evidence. Our knowledge of early Icelandic law depends pretty well entirely on two large collections preserved in two handsome codexes, known respectively as *Konungsbók* and *Staðarhólsbók*, written in the last third of the thirteenth century, 150 years after the composition of Hafliði's screed. I should of course acknowledge in passing that there is a good deal of legal action in numerous sagas with settings in the tenth and early eleventh century, but their accounts can hardly be counted individually reliable as caselaw. If their descriptions agree with laws in the codexes just mentioned – the laws collectively referred to by the old misnomer, *Grágás* – we are none the wiser; and if they disagree, we lack criteria to distinguish what might be from an old, deviant source and what depends on an author's artistry or ignorance. But the

---

[9] *First Grammatical Treatise*, ed. Einar Haugen (2nd ed., 1972), 12, 32; *The First Grammatical Treatise*, ed. Hreinn Benediktsson (1972), 208, 246.
[10] *Gunnlaugs saga ormstungu*, ch. 4; ed. Sigurður Nordal og Guðni Jónsson, Íslenzk Fornrit III (1938), 60; *Færeyinga saga*, ch. 57; ed. Ólafur Halldórsson (1987), 134; *Íslendinga saga*, ch. 39; ed. Jón Jóhannesson, Magnús Finnbogason og Kristján Eldjárn, Sturlunga saga I (1946), 283.

stories do introduce us to medieval Icelanders' notions of equity, something not to be expected in the laws, and sometimes ameliorate the laws' strict view of matters such as intention and liability. They also reveal that law could be manipulated: but that is a lesson we have all learnt nearer home.

Put together, and supplemented by various manuscript scraps, the collections make a formidable body of law. It has long been thought likely that their assembled texts were the result of political interest, associated in some way with the discussions that preceded and followed the Icelanders' decision to accept the overlordship of the Norwegian king, by the pact finally agreed in 1264, discussions doubtless kept alive into the 1270s because of the abortive attempt to introduce a new king-given lawbook in that decade. Normal resort to law had doubtless been curtailed in the turbulent times of the mid-thirteenth century, when violent and ambitious chieftains had the upper hand over law-abiding men. Facing a radical constitutional move about 1260, influential men wanted to gather together the laws of the nation in order to borrow their authority in negotiations with the Norwegian leaders. These may be plausible circumstances but they remain entirely conjectural. We do not know where the editorial work to produce the *Grágás* collections was undertaken, but evidently in scriptoria where earlier copies of law-texts existed or could easily be gathered up. Those copies doubtless varied in quality and extent and most were probably copies of copies of copies, although sometimes the language of an extant text suggests a twelfth-century exemplar. Dateable references are few. Observance of the feast-day of St Þorlákr of Skálholt, for instance, was made law in 1199, that of St Jón of Hólar in 1200; observance of Þorlák's translation in 1237. Amendments to the kinship degrees within which marriage was lawful were introduced as law in 1217, the outcome of decisions of the 1215 Lateran Council. Absence of these provisions in a text would be taken to indicate an origin before those dates, but they were of course items easily inserted in a law record that was otherwise archaic. It will be an absorbing task for a philologist to delve down through the scribal layers and lay bare some foundations. I sometimes regret that I have not spent my fifty years in this game doing just that – half a century would be just about long enough – rather than indulging in other more frivolous pursuits. And there is ample scope for work by the comparative legal historian, who could and should be asked to assess where possible the degree of native independence manifested in different parts of the Icelandic system.[11]

Vígslóði, the section on homicide singled out for mention by Ari, is extant in both *Konungsbók* and *Staðarhólsbók*. The *Konungsbók* text is one of the longest sections in that codex, some 12,000 words, and if we take in additional matter from *Staðarhólsbók* we have a text-mass of something like 16,000 words – the lot would take four or more hours to read aloud. Somewhere in these texts we must have the contents of the homicide section of Hafliði's screed, but we cannot delineate them; and where a law is marked as a *nýmæli*, a new provision, we are in no position to put a date on it. We can however safely assume that procedures remained unaltered, for it is a standard feature of Icelandic law-statement that for a given offence the penalty is laid down and the means of proof prescribed; where appropriate, permissible defence proofs are also listed. Cases, necessarily preceded by publishing and/or summoning, were heard before groups of nominated judges. Means of proof were eye- and ear-witnesses and, as a universal feature, verdicts delivered by a panel of neighbours, five or nine, depending on the nature of the suit. Oaths were sworn by every participant. Strict attention was paid to proper preparation and witnesses to every step in procedure were obligatory. The standard penalties in the developed system were the three-mark fine, lesser outlawry – that is confiscation of property and three-year banishment from Iceland – and full outlawry, which made the culprit an outcast and was virtually a death-sentence. In private law cases various penalty payments were also stipulated, for default or recalcitrance, for example. The court system on these lines, with adversarial confrontation, proved a supple invention which was further prescribed for the resolution of various kinds of local dispute.

---

[11] An interesting step in this direction has recently been taken by Wolfgang Gerhold in his *Armut und Armenfürsorge im mittelalterlichen Island*, Skandinavische Arbeiten 18 (2002).

Opinions have naturally differed about the nature of all this legislation but over the past century the view that has carried most weight has been that of the great *Grágás* editor, Vilhjálmur Finsen. He concluded that the *Grágás* texts were not any straightforward record of customary law; they were not a series of tracts privately composed by law-learned men; nor of course could they depend on judge-made law in any way – the bulk of them fundamentally represented positive law-giving with the authority of the Law Council behind it.[12] It is however hard to believe that every clause had been considered and ratified by the Law Council; and more attention should doubtless be paid to the contributions of law-learned men, men of the stamp of those engaged with Hafliði and Bergþórr in the deliberations of 1117 or those five or more called on to assist a Lawspeaker who found his grasp of any section of the law inadequate for a proper rehearsal of it.[13] They might be compared in their remote way to the jurists of Rome, whose role as "subordinate law-makers" is acknowledged;[14] and we may think that the formulation and elaboration of the laws that ultimately found their way onto vellum were the deposit of their ingenious minds as well of their capacious memories. The typical introduction, *þat er mælt í lǫgum várum*, "It is prescribed in our laws . . .", was an easily adopted formula, and when the framing is largely casuistic, "if so-and-so, then so-and-so", an enquiring or sportive intelligence could be readily prompted to consider another contingency and add another "if" clause to the series; or a thinking man might be led to insert comment or to deduce a general rule from articles just enumerated, though there are not many utterances of this kind in *Grágás* laws. We are also told that where law-texts differed, the one to follow was the one "which says it at greater length in words that affect the case at issue".[15] Development by accretion and expansion is a possibility to be reckoned with.

---

[12] His conclusions are summarily expressed in the Efterskrift printed in *Grágás*, Fjerde Del (1870), 218–21 (in the 1974 reprint included at the end of *Grágás* I).

[13] *Grágás* I, Første Del, 209; *Laws of Early Iceland* I, 188.

[14] Alan Watson, *Roman Law and Comparative Law* (1991), 114–15.

[15] *Grágás* I, Første Del, 213: *er lengra segir þeim orðum er máli skipta með mǫnnum*; *Laws of Early Iceland* I, 190.

There is a fragmentary manuscript, AM 315 D fol., which is among the oldest surviving Icelandic vellums, commonly dated to the second half and most probably to the third quarter of the twelfth century.[16] We might reckon its exemplar was written no more than twenty years or so after Hafliði's screed. The fragments preserve bits of the section of the laws dealing with land-claims, land-use and ownership rights. In *Konungsbók* the whole section is about one-third as long again as the homicide section, in *Staðarhólsbók* it is more than twice as long; both include passages closely corresponding to the text preserved in 315 D fol.[17] The translation I now read from this earliest source keeps close to the clause structures of the Icelandic. The situation envisaged is that of a man who has come to maturity and wants to repossess inherited landed property which has been disposed of while he was still a ward and his affairs looked after by a guardian. We have no idea how often such a situation arose, but since the associated rules are rational and the procedures practical, we may believe that they were called forth by real contingency and were not an imaginative exercise. A claimant was required to publish his claim at the end of one summer's General Assembly as a case he proposed to prosecute for judgment at the Assembly a year later. In this second year:

> He is to call nine neighbours at the assembly, those who live nearest the estate, to give a verdict on whether or not his father owned that estate on his dying day, or the man from whom he inherited did so, and name him and the estate. And if the panel gives a verdict that the man from whom he inherited owned the estate at that time, then the estate must be adjudged to him unless the man who had care of the ward's property can bring a legal defence. This man is to call for a clearing verdict from five neighbours drawn from the prosecution panel, those who live nearest the estate, to give a verdict on whether debts cumbered that estate or not, or whether dependents were a charge on the means or not, so that the capital would diminish. If that verdict is given in his favour, then the man

---

[16] Printed *Grágás* I, Anden Del, 219–26; cf. *Grágás* III (1883), xxxvi–xxxvii. On the dating see Harald Spehr, *Der Ursprung der isländischen Schrift und ihre Weiterbildung bis zur Mitte des 13. Jahrhunderts* (1929), 170, n. 1; his conclusion, "Am besten setzt man sie in das 3. viertel des 12. jh.", is accepted in *Ordbog over det norrøne prosasprog. Registre* (1989), 441.

[17] For the text of the following translated passage see *Grágás* I, Anden Del, 221–22; cf. *Grágás* I, Anden Del, 76–78; *Grágás* II (1879), 414–15; *Laws of Early Iceland* II, 97–99.

> asserting the claim is to call the same five neighbours [to give a verdict on whether] full value was met by full payment or not. If the panel gives a verdict that [full value had not been met by full payment, then the defender has the right to ask] the same neighbours to give a verdict on whether the estate was sold at the best price that could be got or not. If the panel gives a verdict that he sold at the best price he could get, then he keeps the estate unless the claimant argues the case further. Then the man asserting the claim is to call for a verdict on whether he was better off with the estate sold as it was or unsold. If the panel gives a verdict that he was better off with it sold, then he is to call for another verdict on whether there were tenant farms to sell, or rights in other men's land, so that nevertheless cash or capital could have been kept in the main estate though it remained unsold. If the panel gives a verdict that there were tenant farms or rights in other men's land so that means enough would have been to hand if they were sold first, then the estate reverts to the man asserting the claim but otherwise not . . .

And we learn later that the man who irresponsibly first sold the estate was liable to a penalty of lesser outlawry at the suit of the claimant to whom the land reverts and at the suit of the man who first bought it from him; and there were more rules to follow if there had been a chain of subsequent owners.

Now the passage I quoted may sound quite a mouthful, but it is in reality precise, deliberate, technical prose, with enough defining clauses to make it clear which party is involved at any stage and at once flexible enough and emphatically repetitive enough to take the legal moves forward step by step.

This style is the manner of the *Grágás* laws in general but also the manner of the two other *Grágás* sections whose written existence may be taken for granted from their first acceptance. They are the Tithe Law and the general laws relating to Christian observance, the first composed 20 years before Hafliði's screed, the second codified ten years or so after it. We might note too that, although both these sets of regulations were of clerical origin, they were the law of the land and the procedures and penalties prescribed in them were those of the ordinary courts, for dereliction of clerical duties as well as for secular offences. The same style must obviously have been that of Hafliði's screed itself. These texts from either side of 1100 help to bridge the gap between the twelfth century when literate law predominated and the pre-literate age when laws were preserved in the minds of men and transmitted by word of mouth. Can we avoid the conclusion that the laws of that early oral age were also in a similar "dense and business-like" style? It would take us too far afield to explore that possibility, but it is clear enough that the progressive formality and repetition would be aids to memory, and the court procedures, means of proof and penalties were in their way automatic responses. That the existence of such legal prose and widespread knowledge of it might be of material assistance in the development of a lucid, orderly narrative prose, capable of introducing many names of people and places and describing action concisely and graphically – the prose, that is, of the thirteenth-century kings' sagas and sagas of Icelanders – seems to me highly probable. There is no single answer to the question, "What were the origins of Icelandic literature?", but I would count the contribution of the law-framers, law-learners and law-recorders from early times a significant element.

And so we come at last to 1117 in England. According to the *Chronicle*, not much happened that twelvemonth. King Henry spent the year fighting in France while his English subjects suffered, in time-honoured fashion, from heavy taxes and atrocious weather. I have to confess however that 1117 here is a surmise, though not a wild one. There is a Latin text known as *Leges Henrici primi*, Laws of Henry the First, which has long been of interest to legal historians. Needless to say, they are not laws issued by King Henry, but they are from his time, and he and his queen, Matilda, figure in the proem. Matilda died in 1118, so the *Leges* were composed before then. After suitable deliberation, Professor Downer, their most recent editor, decided that the likeliest period for their completion was 1116 to 1118.[18] Even I could see that between 1116 and 1118 there were not many years to choose and I gratefully settled on the obvious one. So 1117 may not be quite exact but it is certainly near enough for my modest purpose.

The author of the *Leges* is identified as the man who made, or started to make, the work known as *Quadripartitus*, the first part of which consists of translations of Anglo-Saxon laws. When he got into the second book of the four he originally planned he gave up and embarked on the *Leges* instead, drawing on his translations and other sources to present a selection of laws which he regarded

---

[18] *Leges Henrici Primi*, ed. L. J. Downer (1972), 36.

as applicable, or desirably so, in his own day.[19] The *Leges* are considered a substantial work for their time, but the whole book is only about as long as the homicide section in *Grágás*. The author mixes his law statements with sententious remarks and maxims and he progresses more by association of ideas than by systematic principle. On the other hand, he is willing to apply scholastic distinctions and to introduce more abstract classifications. The kind of legal thinking evident in the *Leges* is quite unlike that of the Icelandic legislation where enumeration and definition almost always serve only practical ends.

The author of the *Leges* made eclectic use of sources, mostly Anglo-Saxon laws, particularly Cnut's, which he had translated in the *Quadripartitus*, but it is reckoned that ten percent of his material is not of English origin at all. He quotes Augustine and Isidore, decretals and Frankish codes. His scope is also restricted, with very little reference to inheritance or land-law. I was momentarily cheered to find the following passage in the *Leges* which appeared to be consideration of a claim for inherited land now in someone else's possession,[20] a situation comparable to that found in the passage I read just now from AM 315 D:

> A person who is proceeded against with respect to his inherited property shall, after he has reached the age of fifteen years, have an advocate to represent him or himself appear in defence; and he shall bring a charge in respect of his possessions in order that no one may remain in occupation of them for a year and a day without being challenged, while he is of sound health and there is peace in the country . . .

– only to share Dr Wormald's disappointment on discovering that "What ought to be precious evidence of early English inheritance law . . . was lifted almost word for word from *Lex Ribuaria*" – that is, from the laws of the Franks east of the Rhine codified in the seventh century.[21] There is no need to elaborate on the difference

---

[19] See *Leges Henrici Primi*, 5, 17–20; Patrick Wormald, *Legal Culture in the Early Medieval West* (1999), 81–114; idem, *The Making of English Law* I (1999; pb. 2001), 236–66, 407–14, 465–71.

[20] *Leges Henrici Primi*, 184–85 (§ 59, 9a).

[21] *The Making of English Law* I, 414.

between this vague statement of principle, hedged with opaque conditionals, and the brisk squad-drill of the Icelandic regulations.

Before making brief comparison of other salient features, I may say that there are some articles in the *Leges* which remind us of Scandinavian laws and may help to confirm their relative antiquity in the North: the levelling oath, for instance, known from mainland Scandinavian laws, by which a man accepting compensation is face-savingly assured by his opponent that he too would accept compensation in the same circumstances; or the idea that it was ignominious to go on accepting atonement for injury without forceful retaliation, a practice which the Norwegian Gulathing law specifically limited.[22]

The complexity of the English legal situation and of English society comes out clearly in the *Leges*. The author recognises the laws of Mercia and the Danelaw alongside those of Wessex, though he considers the last to be the ultimate arbiter, but he also refers to different practices in Kent and London and leaves some points to be settled by unspecified local custom. All this, of course, is not surprising, given centuries of Anglo-Saxon settlement, more recent Scandinavian invasion, and now new conquest by Normans. He knows three main classes above the unfree, 1200 shilling men, 600 shilling men, and 200 shilling men, with six of the last kind killed in fit revenge for one of the first kind. Local units, tithings, were made responsible for every member of that division of the hundred. Most men were expected to have a lord and lords had overlords; they took their dues when their men were involved before the law. Ownership of land could confer jurisdictional rights in the same way as comital office, and manorial courts could exist alongside the monthly hundred moots and the twice-yearly shire and borough moots. Procedures were largely based on status, compurgation and ordeal, including trial by battle. Cases were heard by few judges, lords, bishops, officers of the crown, other men of

---

[22] *Leges Henrici Primi*, 142–43 (§ 36, 1d); 144–45 (§ 39,1). Cf. references s.v. *jafnaðareiðr* in Johan Fritzner, *Ordbog over Det gamle norske Sprog* II (1891), 220–21; *Den eldre Gulatingslova*, ed. Bjørn Eithun, Magnus Rindal, Tor Ulset (1994), 120 (§ 186): *Nv a engi maðr rett a sér oftarr en þrysvar . . . ef hann hemnisc eigi a milli.*

standing, and the author of the *Leges* can sometimes urge them to weigh circumstances, use discretion and show compassion. Above all was what the author calls "the formidable authority of royal majesty", and a long list of pleas reserved to the crown shows how much to do with law and order, and the profits their maintenance might bring, lay in the king's grasp.

All this may serve to set the simplicity of the Icelandic legal and social situation in stark relief. Within a century of settlement the Icelanders agreed on a constitution with organised local assemblies and a national assembly under the leadership of chieftains; and they agreed on a national law – there is no reference or deference to local custom anywhere in the *Grágás* corpus, though the local communes called *hreppar* could make their own rules as long as they did not clash with anything laid down by the General Assembly. The chieftains were surprisingly many in number, thirty-nine by the end of the tenth century, an oligarchy, if you like, but one which maintained a consensual equilibrium and out of which in the early period arose no single leader or princely family. Every householder with means above a certain level was required by law to join the following of one of these chieftains. They were the *þingfararkaupsbændr*, required to attend assemblies or contribute to the expenses of those who did. A man would generally find it expedient to attach himself to the chieftain who lived closest, but in theory it was a free contract and circumstances or interest might lead a householder to lend his allegiance to a chieftain in another part of the country. In this client relationship every member of a household followed the householder's lead. A census probably made in the 1090s gave the total number of *þingfararkaupsbændr* as 38 hundred, 3800 if the hundred was decimal, 4560 if the hundred was duodecimal.[23] If the average following of a chieftain was thus either a little under or something over one hundred householders, it is clear that any political predominance was impossible without alliances and cooperation; and it was in this relatively static and well-balanced political situation that Iceland's early laws found their development. Thus, while the chieftains formed the nucleus

---

[23] *Íslendingabók*, ch. 10; ed. Jakob Benediktsson (1968), 23 and n. 5 there.

of the Law Council and nominated judges to sit in the courts established at assemblies, their function in judicial process was otherwise limited and they were as liable at law as any other individual. According to the law a general equality was moreover acknowledged. In numerous cases of wrong-doing so-called "personal compensation" was due from the offender to the offended, irrespective of legal penalties, and that sum was the same for every free person, no more for a chieftain than for an ordinary household man. That of course does not mean that individuals were not differently valued when cases came to arbitration and private settlement – many cases were doubtless compounded in that way and they make the stuff of stories. Compurgation as a means of proof hardly existed in Icelandic procedures and, as noted earlier, the main mechanism was the verdict of a panel of neighbours. Ordeal was restricted to paternity suits, and single combat as a means of establishing right had been abolished soon after the acceptance of Christianity in the year 1000. The judges in Icelandic courts were numerous, probably thirty-six in the courts held at the General Assembly, usually twelve in other courts; they could be challenged on various grounds and replaced if necessary. Judgments required a large majority but not total unanimity. On the other hand, there was no room for discretion: if the procedures laid down were properly observed, then judgment in accordance with the law must follow as the night the day; and as we recall, penalties are part and parcel of *Grágás* law-statements.

Penalties – how and by whom were they exacted? There the copious *Grágás* laws leave almost a blank sheet. They lay down rules for payment of fines and for the conduct of confiscation courts when men were outlawed and they offer reward in various contexts. But there was no executive to take action in case of default or defiance: self-help, determined avengers, public opinion, the backing of chieftains with an armed following, all or any of these might be necessary to give effect to a court judgment, but the laws make no overt provision for them. This absence of any organised law-enforcement may at least in part explain the deterrent severity of the punishments envisaged. Fines were not necessarily very damaging but the obligatory sentence for many faults was confiscation of property and three-year exile – no light matter.

Equally the diffuse nature of legal authority in the country and the lack of a permanent magistracy may help to explain why the Icelanders at an early stage elaborated their laws in such detail and often with such pedantic precision. *Jónsbók*, the law-book which superseded *Grágás* laws in 1281, has generally much briefer rules, but their application was backed by a hierarchy of royal officials, up to the king himself.

We may be sure that the constitutional and procedural rules embodied in the laws were hammered out in the first century of the settlement by leaders who preferred peace to strife and when much was doubtless owed to the legal genius of a few men. But it is a more than plausible conclusion that, in the form we know them, the *Grágás* laws were generally elaborated after the conversion and in the course of the eleventh century. That this happened with the influential encouragement of the bishops, primarily Ísleifr and Gizurr, must also follow. The laws are the laws of a Christian country: the church calendar is carefully observed in citing days allowed for legal action, canon law rules on kindred and affinity in marriage are fully applied, the bishop has the final decision in various family matters, spiritual kinship gives grounds for challenge of judges, oaths of course are sworn on a holy book or a cross. About 1070 Adam of Bremen wrote about Ísleifr Gizurarson's stay with Archbishop Adalbert of Hamburg some fifteen years earlier and remarked that the Icelanders regarded their bishop as a king. Then he modified this in a scholion, *Apud illos non est rex, nisi tantum lex* – "Among them there is no king except the law alone."[24] I think Adam was wiser than he knew.

Well, I have swept the pulpit, rehearsed well-known facts and offered comment which largely repeats what I have written earlier and – of course without acknowledgment – what other men of greater learning have written too. That is perhaps not so remarkable in this day and age when a good deal of scholarship in the Norse-Icelandic field appears to be devoted to the rediscovery of things which our nineteenth-century predecessors knew already. And

---

[24] *Gesta Hammaburgensis ecclesiae pontificum*, ed. B. Schmeidler (3rd ed., 1917), 273 (IV, xxxvi; Schol. 156).

finally I comfort myself, and leave you with thanks for your patience, by recalling St Jerome's anecdote about his teacher, Donatus, a famous grammarian but not a man noted for originality. Commenting in class on Terence's *The Eunuch*, he came to the Prologue's well-known line, *Nihil est dictum, quod non sit dictum prius* – "There's naught been said that's not been said before" – and at that burst out with *Pereant qui ante nos nostra dixerunt*, or in Canon Kelly's idiomatic version, "So to hell with those who've said what I say before me."[25] I can only hope that a hundred years hence some bright scholar, in circumstances similar to mine, will find it appropriate to consign me to the same purgatory.

---

[25] J. N. D. Kelly, *Jerome* (1975), 11; Jerome, *Commentarium in Ecclesiastes*, in *Patrologia Latina* XXIII, 1074; *Corpus Christianorum, Series Latina* LXXII, 390.